The World Through My Eyes

Michael Franklin

Contents

Passion

Progression has always been my favorite thing to since I can remember. It's something about building on a thing to make it better that has always excited. I hate sitting still. I guess I'm hyperactive.

I HOPE I DONT CHOKE

My body is shaking from being nervous and so excited all in one,
What a great feeling it is to be scared and anxiously waiting for a certain situation
to come,
Going over the words over and over and over in your mind,
Hoping when the time presents itself your tongue won't go numb,
Will I be liked or will I be rejected,
It's like, Oh no, is that the "Bright Light", but on the other hand it must be heaven,
It's like eating a lot of ice cream and knowing that you are going to get a brain
freeze,
The moment is quickly coming, but it's taking too long, "What do I do?" Man this
is getting too heck-ted,
These two emotions are rapidly flowing through every vain in my body,
I thinking when will this be over, like when your first child is learning how to use the
potty,
It's nice outside and I can't stop and enjoy this beautiful day,
Now I want to get out of this, like a Snicker's commercial, I just want to get away,
My heart beat is pounding and got me feeling like every nerve in my body is
broken,
Twitching, shaking, anticipation, and whole lot of nervous hoping,

I wish I was a big company that ended in INC., so I could sit back and do all the talking
through my spokesman,
I'm on a ship right now about ready to sink, and all I can think of is the worst way
to die for me would be by choking.

M.M.Franklin

Stairsteps

S eeing a path progressing to get to the end,
T rying to move from obstacles to better yourself,
A glance back only to stay humble and remember where it is from
Which you come,

I ts not a horrible thing to but your pride to the side and ask for

Alittle help,

R eally believe and trust in the power within,

S teps are not just for reaching another level but can be the beginning
Of progression,

T wo, one, a million all are means to get to a end,

E very step has a purpose and within it an important lesson,
P eople grow like stairsteps from a baby to become an adult,
S tay on the path, the destination is the meat, so treasure your
Memories of every step, cause its the salt.

M.M.Franklin 1/11/11

P.L.O

Wow, I don't know where you came from, like snow days, you got no class so why are testing me,
I'm trying to grow towards the sun like a plant, and you're trying to hold me down, its like your stalking me,
Never ending hurdles, soon as I clear you and get one foot to the ground, you reappear, here we go again,
I'm always on the defense around you, you are an offensive guard trying to block me from tackling my dreams,
I'm putting down how I feel about you, but some how you're drying up the ink, hold up let me get anothet pen,
Ok, I'm back at it and thank you for constantly reminding me that things aint always what it seems,
I feel like Malcolm X when I see you cause I got to get past you by any means,
Its very necessary for me not to stop I got to keep pushing forward,
Give me the strength to overcome these P.L.O.'s in my life, Please and Thank You Lord,
Your nominated for the most hindering and destructive, causing people to fail, but
don't go up on the stage cause in my life you won't get that award,
But you get a honorable mention cause you tried your best, I mean you tried your worst,
You make me stronger, without you I probably wouldn't have made it this far, you're like my gift and my curse,
This is about someone or something that always does something to hold you down or tries to make you lose focus,
Use these Permanent Lifetime Obstacles for practice to make you stronger,
Because there will be times in your life where everything around is falling down and you need to hold on to what's inside of you alittle while longer.

What I am

I need some nourishment,

Taught to do it on my own,
Been thinking for myself ever since,

Learned how to express poetically,

I want to read and write a whole lot more,
I try not to let the little things upset me,

This is the time I claim my spot,

Years ahead of my age,
I'm the sun in my galaxy, get your sunglasses, too bright, get some pot holders,
you can't hold me I'm too hot.

My Year

This is my year!

I won't be stopped, I'm so focused,
This is my year!
All your petty attempts to try and stop me will turn up hopeless,
This is my year!
I'm laughing at you like I'm in a comedy show, cause you're what the is,

This is my year!

Sorry, you've been sent here to block my vision, but it didn't work I didn't notice,

This is my year!

I'm keeping you far away from my thoughts, this is called my solstice,

This is my year!

Go find someone else to bother.

I will never quit

I was tried of my life so I decided that I got to make a change,

So that comes with some readjustments and a lot of pain,
I'll do what it takes for everyone around me to live better,
I keep telling everyone that I have no twin, I'm not the same,
Continuously looking after those around, that's all I know
I'll never quit,
Still keep my head up looking in the skies,
When I was young I had to many whiping that makes it hard for me to sit,
Still, if it takes all of them, I'll use my lives,
People that come in contact with me, like a robber with a conscience, just want
To give me up,
Cause they find out they can't transform me, I'm more than meets the eyes,
Before, my life was like a black cat eaten a bad apple, rotten luck,
My thoughts keep growing like some grass after it rains, but I gotta maintain
My focus, cut through the weeds,
And just because I can see my destination ahead, I can't stop now, got to keep running, like a Fresh cut when it bleeds,
And I can get as deep as the ocean, but I told my teacher I'm not the average, I
Don't like these C's,
But she gave them to me anyway,
So the determination makes me want to make my life beautiful even when I
Face gloomy days,
And I'm no star but there is a little
Twinkle in each one of my eyes that represents my little girls,
Their my world, welcome I'm the host, there is no hostess but my girls are
Sweet like cinnamon swirls,
And if you don't hear me yet.
I treat my problems in my life like a 2 min workout, no sweat.

Brain

My mind left a long time ago, I don't think right,
Alot of people walk mentally, I like to take flights,
Explore my horizons,
I want to blanket my brain, like the coverage at Verizon,
I train it everyday hoping one day I can let it off the leash,
Alot of things to learn out there, I'm hungry and I'm looking at all
    This knowledge like its a feast,
The brain is amazing,
True powers of it is shocking, like a police officer when they do their
    Tazing,
Mind over matter,
Without knowledge my mind gets weak, its like trying to hold your bladder.

M.M.Franklin 1/15/11

FAN

As I look up and stare at this fan going in circles, it kinda reminds me
Of me,
My lifes pattern all captured in one motion,
The way its spinning crazy without going nowhere, it just wants to be
Free,
Free like a bird, or boat in the middle of the ocean,

Unappreciated for the good it does, but you're quick to complain when

Its broke and can't do anything,
You see, I don't think this fan asked to be here and try to comfort
World, but still it does, this fan its just like me,
Going clockwise, doing what everyone wants me to do, like a robot,

Going counter-clockwise, going against the flow, why am I not able

To say what I think without sour looking faces,
Well one thing is different, you think I'm going to sit around and
Keep allowing someone to keep turning me on and off at the flick

Of a switch, I think naught,

Well maybe you'll appreciate me when you see I'm not there and
You're sweating, with wet clothes, and uncomfortable because
The room temperature has gotten too hot,
Or maybe not.

M.M.Franklin 12/22/10

COMFORT

Man, this bed is comfortable, this couch is comfortable,

But I got get up and take care of things that need to be,
I feel like a cheetah in a six foot cage, complacency is killing me,
Man, this bed is comfortable, this couch is comfortable,
But it's alot of things I need to do today to get where I want to be

Tomorrow,

Somebody please tell me the difference between comfortable and

Prison, the gap is so so very narrow,

Man, this bed is comfortable, this couch is comfortable,

Why on earth would someone make these things like this,

It's like as soon as you lay on one, you fall into a very deep and dark

Abyss,

Man, this bed is killing me, this couch is killing me,

I got to get up!

M.M.Franklin 12/22/10

NIGHTLY QUESTION of MINE

Ever since I could remember, something in me has been telling me that
I'm here for something great,
So I have nightly conversations with destiny, complaining, saying
"Where are you, you're kinda late!"
Then destiny puts me back in my place and says, "Who are you, you
Can't rush fate,
Sit back and show some respect for the process and the timing it
Takes.",
I do like to practice patients, but man this is killing me,
Its hard with these infinite thoughts running through my head
Continuously,
My eyes aren't great, wear glasses occasionally, but I see clearly
With these visions of mine,
So what do I do? Try to cut to get ahead of the line,
Or do act like a thief, black mask, black gloves, and just take some
Time?

M.M.Franklin 12/11/10

Motivated, Dedicated

I'm highly motivated, highly dedicated,

To do what I need to, to take care of the people around me,
Even if it means the people around me can't be right around me,
I feel like I have to go through the door first to make sure its alright,
But then again, I feel as though I have to go in last to make sure everyone gets in safe,
I don't think like the majority, I might be from outer space,
I go through it, in life, just so you song have to,
If someone ever tried you, don't worry I speak mostly through my actions, so you won't have to,
And I don't get any pleasure from the things of this world,
I get my enjoyment from seeing all of you happy,
I found the last bottle of oil on this Earth, you can use it I'll stay nappy,
You won't believe how quickly your life can change positively, if you're determined,
In the last few months I feel like I have reached out and touched the sun, without the burn,
They say knowledge is power, but real power comes from using that knowledge, that's really what you should learn,
My minds full of ideas and goals,
I'm highly motivated, highly dedicated,
I feel like its the birthday of a renewed soul, celebrate!
There is something in me, there is something in you, our minds are like credit cards, unlimited with power, call the number and activate it,
I'm here for you, all of you,
I'm a 24-hour super store where everything is free, I don't need nothing to be returned,
I just need a smile when I'm driving this bus load through life, that's what will keep me going, that's all the fuel I need to burn,

In highly motivated, highly dedicated,
I was formed from clay, but I got a heart of steel you
can't manipulate it,
Why? Because I'm highly motivated, highly dedicated.

I believe I am king

I want to walk and talk like, I believe that I am king,
You see, I believe if you trace my lineage back far enough you'll see
That I am connected to a great line of royalty,
But even if you didn't, even if you couldn't, I don't need that to tell
Me that I am great,
This blood inside me is so thick, so strong, it feels like a solid, I don't
Know how it passes thru my veins,
I believe that I am here forever, after all that is how long a true king
Reins,
I want to walk and talk like, I believe that I am king,
No, not like Martin Luther or that one who blues is what he sings,
But a king to help open up closed eyes, fight mental battles, and
Carry this world on my back, this is what I was born for,
One day I will rise, be the voice that shakes and rattles, the rails that
Keeps this world on track, this is what I'm here for,
Because I walk and talk like, I believe I am king...
Where's my crown, my throne, somebody get me my scepter,
I'm ready to do my thing!

My Pencil

It brings out the best in me, brings out the worst in me, my truest
Thoughts and feelings come out,
I can be tired or have some place to go but its like a battery in my
Hand and keeps it going across the page, couldn't stop if I wanted to,
No matter if its a number one, number two, or binary code, that
Doesn't matter as much as the story its told,
Over a million years old, age is really unknown, but you can tell its
Been around because of all the wisdom it has produced,
An honor just to hold it in my hands, it has created masterful works
Of art throughout history,
Sometimes I feel like it makes people who normally wouldn't, sit
Down a listen to me,
Sometimes it makes me listen, it mirrors back to me, my inner
Vision,
Sometimes it get deep inside me and shows the pain I have
through a little pen like incision,
But for all the ugly things its shows me and all the beautiful things
That come out,
It sometimes makes me understand why I had to go that route,
Get it in my hands and like a piece of velcro, like a close love that's
Leaving out of town, it's hard to let it go,
But I gotta keep going, making these letters form these words that to
Some people might seem odd, but to me they always seem to
Even.... Me out.

My Journey

I don't know where my life is heading, but I plan for it to end up
Right,
Everyone one I ever cared about has been taken away or left, I guess
I'm a repelling magnet,
I know it's for a reason, but still with my torn meniscus, I can't stand
It,
I tell you for all of them, I can't quit now, my eyes are getting better
I see great things in my site,
Even if its full, I don't care, I'm getting on now, I don't want to catch
The next flight,
This journey is dark and I was told I have a light inside, and it would
Brighten my way if I showed it, even if a small fragment,
I am now focused, it's real simple, me plus obstacles pulling me off
My path is real problematic,
I once heard, shoot for the moon if you miss you be amongst the
Stars,
You can come with me if you're not afraid of heights,
A voice inside me keeps telling me,
Stay on the path, keep straight, I know you're going thru it right now
But pretty soon it will be alright,
So I clinch my teeth, walk hard, keep my head up, and move forward,
Greatness is my belief, distractions I have no regard, a focus drink
Is in my cup, and one more thing to say, onward.

Locomotive Style

My style is locomotive,
Wildly pushing forward, I'm a loco in motion,

There ain't no slowing down, I'm allergic to coasting,
If you ain't on my team then get off my track,
Headed full speed with no looking back,
Like a roller coaster ride so hold on to your hat,

Don't need no one's coal, I fuel off my own fire within,

My desire is strong, if I fail, better believe I'm trying again,
Only one body, but I got the heart of ten men,
My locomotive style, there ain't no stopping it.

AWAKE

The mornings air is cool and clean, gives us strength to rise to our
Feet,
Unbelievable feeling to wake up full again, the previous day drained
Us like we had a crack and all of power and energy leaked,
Out, this vessel of life is now fully renewed and ready for another,

The beautiful sun arises and kisses us to let us know it's time to

Awake from our aggravated or quiet nights slumber,
A new day, time to put our past behind and focus on the future, a
New start,
Rejuvenated, the sun is up, focus on the light and try not to let your

Life be directed by what happened in the dark,

Stretch your mind, not only your body, to see everything that is
Possible for you,
To do more than you previously did, another chance when we step
Out the bed, that is God's gift to you,

So as we take a deep breath while that sun is shining bright,

Try very hard to forgive, I know it's hard to forget what happened last
Night, smile its a new day.

Chasing

This women is incredible, body formed from clay, earth walking
Goddess,
Can't let her get away, I gotta try my hardest,
My heart is pounding so heavily,
I'm walking with confidence to this rhythm, look how her body
Moves to this melody,
Her voice is like a symphony of seduction, like a magnet bringing me
Nearer,
Her smile knocks me out, full blown concussion, to fall and get up
Starts with the man in the mirror,
But the closer I get the harder it becomes for me to grab hold of her,
getting tired from chasing after the sun,
It feels like I started a journey years ago but everyday I wake up to
See that my journey has just begun,
The sum of the situation is adding up to be that she is only a figment
Of my imagination,
Something my brain has cleverly created to keep me chasing,
Representing me chasing everything that I will one day be,
So I guess I'll keep trying to catch up with this incredible woman, all
I know is to go after what I want, but lately something has been
that maybe, just maybe I should just sit back and wait for
Her to come to me.

Energy

I have this burst of energy pulsating deep within my mind and body,
I also close my eyes and feel it all around me, I'm surrounded by this
Vibrant glow,
I'm in the midst of this energy bubble, submerged,
Pure energy circulating through every fiber and throughout every

Vein in my body,

I feel like I can be the source to light up a city, so much power in me,
What am I to do with this force, I want very much and need to know,
So much energy that even when my eyes feel like a hundred pounds, I
Still can't sleep, how good it would be to rest, so I've heard,

Energy, energy, energy!

Its like I'm being tazed and all this voltage of energy is shocking my body,
It's causing my mind to move so fast, and even though its going so
Fast, it still feels like everything around me is moving so very slow,

So I guess I am energy, energy is me, so I just might have my first name

Changed to that word,
Energy.

Family is my number one concern, over myself. If I'm shooting for something big, most likely it's not for me, it's for them. I need nothing but them because they are everything.

Family

Without my family, I would bump into the walls of life, like I'm walking in the dark,

You all are like a bunch of lighting bugs in a jar, that give light to my path,
For my family I would give anything, my brain, my lungs, my kidneys, my last drop of blood, even my heart,
If I had one hundered things, I would give you one hundred things, so what will I be willing to keep for myself, well I'll let you do the math,
Unconditional love, I love you when it's all good, I love you when it's all bad,
If your spine was to go out, you could have mine, and don't worry cause I got your back,
I need you more than you'll ever need me,
You shade me, so my goal is to create an abundance of water to support my family tree,
Wisdom seeps from your trunk, so sweet like sap,
My family is full of comedians, so most of the time I sit back, enjoy the show and just laugh,
I wouldn't sell these memories for a billion dollars,
They're buried deep down inside, and guess what, there is no map,
To have a family like this I don't desrve it,
Even while writing this, there is a battle I must go through inside of me, with all kinds of thoughts and expression,
But I'm pleased to go through it, to be able to give you this gift, because you all are more than worth it.

Message to God

Forgive me for when I didn't try to understand, or was it that I just plain out didn't listen,

Thank you for when the times got tough , you always seems to come by and ease some of the tension,
Forgive me for when I woke up early in the morning, you know what for,
Thank you that I don't have to deal with those situatuons any more,
Thank you for the positive, thank you for the negative,
Because if it wasn't for that, I wouldn't have learned

everything I ever did.

C.A.

There is pain in my heart, so much I can't describe it through words,
And I don't even think I can get out the full feeling through this writing,
I can't hold back, they're running, I can't s stop them, my legs are weak
Not only at the knees, but from my toes to my thighs,
I feel like I've failed them, I would say I love them and would do
Anything for them,
When in actuality, when it came down to prove it, when the real test
Came up, it seem to be just lies,
Because I couldn't stay in a situation that was stressful, I'm

Hyperactive, it's torture for me to stay still,

I feel like being here is the best thing for you,
I feel like being away is the best thing for you,
But I feel like what good am I if I can't move my body and my mind,

Everything happens for a reason right, but if its good then why does it

Hurt so damn bad,
People come and go in your life, everyone has a set time in your life
There are no guarantees,
My legs feel weak right now, but not only in my knees.

Mother 2 B

It's a natural thing like the rotation of the stars,

Like a runner who trains for a race, you spend months getting
your body ready for that one special moment to come,
What you have inside of you will one day brighten up your life,
the same way that you came and brighten up ours,
Right now you have a glow growing inside of you that when
released we will all need sunglasses because that glow is
going to shine brighter then the sun,
Stay focused, buisness first, pleasure second, I know it's hard
work now but when its all done it will be a lot of fun,
We believe in you, believe in yourself,
Your family is here for you, your surrounded by a lot of help,
This world is full of a lot of beautiful and amazing things,
But nothing compares to the joy that a baby brings,
The world goes around and the ocean is deep,
Search inside of yourself for the answers you seek,
Get yourself ready because you are a young mother
    2B.

No Hurry

Beautiful girl so anxious to grow into a grown woman, watching the
  Women walk by,

She sees the nice clothes, make up looking nice, high heel shoes, and

  Hair looking so right,

And she tells herself, "I want to do what I have to do to look like them",

So she copies the talk, put her mothers high heels on and practices
  The walk,

She really doesn't know how they did it, so she exaggerates the thing they

  Did with their hips, gets into her mothers makeup and puts the the

  Whole stick on her lips,

And her face, not knowing that it took some time for them to perfect
These arts,

She doesn't see the hard work these women do on a daily, to get
Those clothes,

The pain they went through before they learned how to walk in
Those heels,

The hours put in, trail and error to get their makeup and hair looking
Right, and still,

Didn't get it quite the way they wanted, quite the style the wanted,

So they take it off, pulled their hair down and start over again,
My point is young girl, it takes time to be a women, and even then
Its still not easy to walk in those shoes,

Enjoy your life as a young beautiful girl, its such a precious time,

Don't do what you see, come up with your own style,
And remember its only right to steal, when you're taking your time.

This is for

This is for my mother, my girl, and my daughters,
This is for my grandmother, aunts, cousins, and my sistas,
Each second I'm away from you, you know its gets harder,
I just left you and already I start to miss ya,
Beautiful black women in my life,
Dark range of complexion but inside them shines all light,
Heaven forbid anyone how tries to hurt ya, there's not a place they hide anywhere on this globe,
I didn't want to, please forgive me, God take care of them is the prayer I'll pray for their soul,
And all the pain you go through as black women,
Pass that on to me like your in a marathon,
And if what you need lies in the middle of the biggest ocean, you know I'm going
swimming,
Your a beautiful melody to me, I dont want it to stop, be my never ending sound,
My black women you have come so far, and because of you I have too,
I live for you, I stay out of jail for you, this poem I write for you,
And if the sky turned black, I'll turn it back blue, there's nothing I wouldn't do,
This is for Cynthia, Betty, and can't forget Nikki,
In this ugly world I close my eyes and picture my black women because ya'll are so pretty,
Debbie, Marika, Jazzy, I love ya'll all,
Intelligent, composed, classy, go get ready, I bought a ticket for everyone to be my date at the
Ball,
I thank you all, my black women, for coming into my life and keeping me sane,
This is for Mira, Ahlora, Camyra, and Louraine,
This is for the women of color who helped strenghten my backbone,
If you needs it, here is my heart, it all yours keep it, no loan,
I love how the sun glistens as it touches all the different skin tones,
If you ever get mentally stressed, rest your thoughts in me, I'm your comfortable home.

I love you,
I'm here for you.

Daddy's Love

You're the angel that I seek,

Without you around me, I feel like Monday thru Sunday, I'm really weak,
But don't worry because day and night I'm workikng out,
Training so I can get stronger, to win this title bout,
And it makes me happy just to see you, and give you a hug, amd hear your voice,
Love the day you were born, now I sit back and watch you grow,
But in reality I'm standing and making moves for you, just thought you should know,
I'm working hard trying to move the gray clouds from out your sky,
And even when I'm not able, and the rains pours, I'll teach you how to maintain and keep your sanity dry,
Because in life, you will always have your problems,
But in becoming successful, when the problems keep adding up, spend some time focusing on how to solve them,
And I have never seen so much talent, compassion, and itteligence bundled up,
Thank you God for these two gifts, so special,
Happy, so I'm full of tears, where's the tissue, I think to myself even if I get sick and began to sneeze, it's ok because God has already blessed you,
These girls are the resaon for my smile,
And the reason why my head is above water when I haven't seen land in awhile,
You're my heart pumping laughter, smiles, love, and joy in my life,
You two are the only reason that I'll ever know what it means to be in love at first sight,
And that's my view,
Camyra and Ahlora, guess what, daddy loves you.

Life is really simpler than many may think. It's composed of things we control and things that we can't control. The hardest thing in life is probably distinguishing between the two, and not dwelling on those things that are out of our hands.

My life,

My pain,
My story drowned in rain,
Black rain, hard and cold,
Can you stomach this food, it's hard and old,
Molded, bitter, and stale,
I never seen the beauties of heaven,
But I swear this world I live in is hell,
You want to know what I think, no it's sacred and not for your ears,
Surrounded by immature thinkers, come back when you gain a couple of years,
Never really struggled with life, but every day I struggle with my thoughts,
The world is getting crazier every day,
I want to fly me and my girls away,
Please Lord give this angel back his wings so I can sore through the wind like a great black hawk.

Untitled

Wisdom seeker, truth seeker,

I want nothing but realness in my life,

No lie I seriously need ya,

Sometimes I take a drink, thru crazy images I fight,
Mentally drained,

Fighting to stay sane,
Life is crazy, I want you to be my shelter from all this pouring rain.

Makes no sense

The right to do what you want to, say what your feeling,
Just to get to the core of that world would be so very appealing,
Not to see so many robots get upset when there is a systems glitch,
Only to see that the way their living is a dream and can't be awaken by a simple pinch,
Mentally in a burning box and your life is desperately gasping for air,
It might be wise to start thinking differently, go cold turkey, because they say it's not healthy to smoke them, so why would you want to keep living in a square.

Beautiful Day

I wake up, open my eyes, and take a deep breath of fresh air,

Get out of bed, pull back the curtains and let the sun shine kiss me,
I get excited because today looks like it's going to be a good day,
I have a lot of goals and can't wait to open the door and face the new challenges awaiting me in the city,
The sun couldn't be a brighter orange, and the grass couldn't be a greener green,
Everything is so clear today, my eyes feel like they're brand new,
Just like the window on your car after you just got it washed, my ind is clear too,
No pains in my body, I'm moving like a well tuned machine,
This is a beautiful day and a work of art,
Like the tower in Piaza that leans,
Hour glass words, I'm running out of words to say,
So like my words, the day is moving on, so let me end this, sit back and enjoy it because today is a beautiful day.

I'm confused

Just leave,
No stay,

Come back,
Go away,
I want you,
I want you to leave,

I'm lying,

Believe me,
You're my life line,
Flat I'm dead,
Stay, go away,
You heard what I said,
You're a pain,
Pain I can't live without,
I'm confused,
Please don't believe the words that are coming out of my mouth.

Lost my left hand

I feel like I just stole something, got caught, and they cut off my left
Hand,
Something I can survive without, but was so accustomed to using
Everyday,
Now everyday tasks seem to take an eternity, it just ain't the same,
I didn't take it for granted, but then again, I did think it would be around forever, man I
miss my left hand,
Even though it's gone and not coming back, I guess you can call it
My calendar thoughts, cause I'll think about it everyday,
And I know my right hand is missing it, like twins, they looked and
Did everything almost exactly the same,
I remember winning in basketball with it, there's nothing like my left hand,
Now doing pushups and pullups is a challenge for me everyday,
I used to do complex things, now I have to stick with the
Elementary,
Because when you look at my arms, one of those things is not like the
Other, one of those things just isn't the same,
And it never will be.

Chills

Man, my body is cold, I got chills right now, what in the world is this
Shit,
I'm so cold that it burns, I need help, somebody come and
Get me up out of this hell pit,
Flying high on life is not good, watch your heads below, this is some
Fowl shit,
Fever, body sore, high temperature, headaches, my head is sick,
This vapor rub of pain is abusing my life, product of Mr. Vick,
Can't cut thru all these thoughts I have with a chain saw, yeah its
That thick,
Walking around pacing, this feels like I just got a beaten and now I
Can't sit,
Horrible aroma in the air is like pain, it's smells like the same shit,
Fred Sanford's the big one, could this be it,
But I gotta to keep going, get focused, look up to the sky for
, this is how I do a face lift,
Lord, what ever else I have to go thru to get where I need to be,
Please help me get thru it.

What is it?

I don't know what love is, but sometimes I feel I should say it,

I don't know what love is, but sometimes I feel I should play it,
Play like I do, play like I know,
Play like love is leading me and I would follow it anywhere it goes,
What is it about, love,
If it exists is it good or is it bad,
They say it makes you smile with happiness, then turns around and makes you cry a river of tears,
To me love is joke because it makes me laugh,
I do believe that love is very consistent, it has continued to bring me pain for most of my years,
I don't think I need love, I need reality, and I need the truth,
That's the only thing I get my joy from because it has never lied to me , has it ever lied to you?
But I would love to love, love to know what love is, and I would love to know why love doen't love unconditionally,
But love is not here, it's just a word that doesn't mean, it doesn't even exist to
me,
Does this make sense to you, do you think it makes sense to me?
Love doesn't,
You tell me what love is and I will tell you what love isn't,
If love was a person I would kill it,
Responsible for so much pain, I can't stand it,
Love is just a word made up that doesn't me shit,
But always seems to shit in everyones life,
Love, what is it?

I thought she knew

I thought she knew me, maybe she doesn't, because if she did then
She would realize that its just as hard to me as it is to her,
No green flashes either, I wake up out of my sleep too to check,
Phone calls missed, zero, and I still have hallucinations of bumping
Into her,
We used to be on a smooth ride with the top down, so now when I look
Over and she's not here, I feel like a wreck,
It's hard for me not to pick up the phone to call and send those
"what u doin" text,
But it makes me want to be with her more, and although I very much
Want it, I know its not good,
So if you hear my silence, then that must mean you hear my pain,
Translate it please,
Life long lessons, you would think I would already know how to
Speak that language, never really got the accent part right,
But I would really like to hear what it is saying, I really would like for
It to tell me how I could ease it alittle, so I can get some sleep at
Night,
It hurts to keep away from someone I thought was a perfect fit,
Before would have thought she understood, guess not, guess I was
Wrong for thinking that she knew me.

Got to get a grip

My insides feel torn right now, going thru some loops,

Tangled, dismantled, If it was a cereal , it would be pain with two scoops,

My feelings and my guts have been spilled all over the floor, oops,
Let me pick them up and put them back inside, recoup,

Get control, can't be losing my grip, that's stupider than that song, Chicken Noodle Soup,
Gotta get like my mom used to say, grounded!, Invisible connection with the earth, bluetooth,
I was feeling like a homeless person in a thunderstorm with no roof,
Now I'm trying to be all I can be like the Army, pay attention, solute!,
It's a war going on inside of me, gotta prepare for battle and strap up my boots,
Treat my life like basketball, keep my eyes on the goal, focus on the hoops,
I'm in control, the CEO of my life, but I rarely wear suits.

Pay Attention

My lady drowns out my negative thoughts, my life guard, she swims well,

Its so cold, let me be your towel as you step out of the jacuzzi,

Kool apple, me minus her equal so sick, God bless,

Education, she taught me how to get over my water phobia,
Feels like I'm in too deep, can't dress them, my thoughts are so naked.

Hard to Forget

It's too hard to forget,
So I'm not going to even try,
The hard days and cold nights we spent,
Not even fearing the possiblity that one day we might die,

I love you like brothers,
Would have done anything for you,
Tight with your siblings, close to your mothers,
I pray for you, cause only God and I know the reasons you do what you do,

Sorry I left in a hurry, the way I did,
I hope one day God helps you understand,
I would have gone crazy if I woke one day to find out you were dead,

Forget I never will, the days in the cut,
The pain in the air,
The girls that braided my hair,
And the bullets we had to duck,

You taught me to be tough, and to fear nothing,
All I need is a heart of steel, and to keep my head up,
Taught me how to survive and think smart,
It was half way empty then you helped fill my cup,

I wish you left with me, but you were addicted to your life,
They talked to rudely, and wonder why we spit back,
Even if it wasn't storming , we couldn't help but hear the thunder,
But things went wrong and now all I can do is look back,

I didn't have a care,
Didn't know what's real,
Smoke filled my air,
I hope one day I will heal,
I knew nothing but pain,
Could hardly see past today,
Feeling nothing but black rain,
The only way to ease it was to play,
Spent my whole life fighting,

Should have started boxing,
Never knew I had a passion for writing,
One day you'll be free too, that's the only song my heart sings,

I miss ya'll,
Forgive them,
Forgive me,
It's hard to forget them.

It's tough out here

I don't believe in giving up but the pressure is
Starting to build up,
Shits getting heavy, I try and I try but every time
I turn around to see where am at, I'm no further
Than when I started,
I'm not complaining, I'm venting. I know it could be
a lot worse, some people can't even pee in a cup,
Much less stand on two feet, I feel like if I didn't
Want to run in this race I should have never even
Started,
I set the bar high, my favorite direction is up,
But recently this pain in my knee won't even allow me
To jump,
This pressure in my head feels like a gorilla is trying
To break out, I'm stressed
I feel like all the hard work I do goes straight to the
Shredder, even when its the best,
Never been a quitter, made some smart decisions
And some dumb ones,
Never been in it for personal reasons, I'll go through
Hell for my loved ones,
I got a family but can't enjoy them with sleepless
Days and tiresome nights,
I've done some fucked up shit in my life, and they
Say what goes around comes around,
But darkness seems to be replacing my light, I help
People even when I can't, I'm making a lot of
Noise but I hear no sound,
Always did and still believe that I am a star, though
I feel dim sometimes,
Tell me have you ever felt so powerful and so
Powerless at the same time,
I truly deeply in my heart believe that I here for something great. LORD please give me a sign.

This Is Me

It's been a minute since I've wrote my last poem, about a day or two,
I love poetry, I like to exercise and take care of my body, but this is a
Way to exercise my mind,
I love thinking, in my head everyday is a lesson in school,
I'm a learner, I like to figure out new ways to do things and take my
Time,
I'm somewhat patient, I don't mind waiting but I need to learn how
To enjoy the process, I know it's a reward in that,
The gift to give is in me, I'll give everything and expect nothing at all,
I want everything, not for me but people around, my back is strong,
You can put your weight on my back,
But the weight of my own thoughts is heavy, I just pray that God
Strengthens my knees so they won't make me fall.

Waking in the cold

It seems like my lifes path right now has got me walking in the cold,
Mind over matter, too many things going on in my brain to realize
That its 10 below 0,
I still believe that I can, I walk in yes, some people like to walk in the
I don't know's,
It's more than me, gotta keep on moving despite these frost beaten toes,
It's a mystery how I'm still moving in this cold weather, and this
Trouble I've seen, when is it going to stop, nobody knows,
Seen alot of warm places on this path, but when I get there the
Doors always slam close,
Forgive me if I seem mean, I had to harden my shell to protect me from
These harsh elements, similarities of a concrete rose,
The weather man said it's was suppose to be nice out side, would
Have dressed better if I knew I would be walking in this cold,
I'm not a napkin or some clothes, don't try me, please
I'm not going to fold,
I'm glad I have too many thoughts going on right now to distract me
From realizing that I'm walking in the cold.

Karma returned

Karma's out there, and bests believe its real,
Purple arms, bruises, and fracture wrists, damn that's hard to
Swallow that pill,

I heard it was a rough day, but I suggest everyone just chill,

Dealing with feelings, that's the hand karma sometimes wills,
Out, of her mind if she thinks I wasn't willing,
Until this, preapproved credit, I had the pen ready to sign on that deal,
I had the chart right up to my face, but still couldn't see the small
Print,

It read, Michael your just a pawn in someone's made up fantasy,

I put alot of trust in someone, asked them to be real with me, now I
Got to go to the eye doctor, I must be blind,"Can you help me see!",

Black sunglasses and cane, I thought I had someone to help me,

But was led into a busy street,

What did I do to deserve it? What ever it was, I guess that's just my

Karma coming back to me.

My Mind Ain't Right

The nights is days, my cold is hard,

The pain in my eyes, my heart shed tears,
Gotta get legs, away go yards,
Positive away, future negative years,
Mind is outrun, can't tired my fears,
Life is breath, scared is precious,
Strong is the light, but the darkness in me is true,
The world, my head keeps chasing, spinning lifes dreams and lessons,
Wisdom find your way thru the tunnel, obstacles you go thru,
Be a star in your own shine, they can right so can you.

Let It Shine Always

When I met you, you got me rolling like the wheel,
My cup had holes, you sealed it up and then filled it up, you said you didn't want me to spill.
How could sumthing so little be like a car wreck and impact my life.
My 1 800 automated service available all day and night.
When your around, complete trust, I'll close my eyes you can be my sight,
Life can be real shitty sometimes, I need to get away,
My life is like a craps game and you're like my paradise.

My Mind Minus Sanity

Since you've been gone, a war has been going on in my head,

I've felt like a sweet potato pie after Thanksgiving, there has been
No peace,
I'm hungry for the mental stimulation that I got from being around
You,

Crazy thoughts seemed to cloud my mind, my mind when you

Were around was so at ease,

And now my head aches, I need an extra strength Excedrin,

Tylenol, Aleve, you are gone but you didn't leave out of my
Thoughts,

Its like my mind is in a vise, can't handle this tension,

I have everything with no air, like I got locked away in a bank volt,
I was in school and learning how to love life, until the principle
Gave me an unnecessary suspension,

You went away, so why does it feel like I'm the one who got locked

Up with no visitations?

Life is like....

Life is like a roller coaster with all is ups and downs,
Bungee cord jumping, a dog that was lost and is now homeward bound,
Back and forth like ping pong, sometimes it is but not as always as
Quick,
Joys and happiness come and go like we're in are in the middle of
A Houdini trick,
Lifes gravitational pull lets you get off your feet, get high and then
Pulls you back,
Like a basketball player that jumps high, you can't stay up there forever
You must come back,
Or like a tug of war match, pulling in each direction,
A girl that likes to tease, getting you excited and leaving you with a worthless erection,
But all worth it, life is sweet like chocolate that melts in your mouth,
It's sad like a mother that has a child that's old enough to move out,
Life is beautiful, frustrating with alot of truth, lies, and dares,
Life is beautiful to share it with when you find someone who really cares.

Lies

It feels like I'm under a pile of bricks, it's too much pressure in this life of mine,

You'll go blind if you could see the pain that I've seen with my eyes,

Faced death in many forms, manys ways, but I survive,
So many decision to deal with it's got my head pounding,
I'm a solider in this life of war, can you hear the trumpets sounding,
Hear the drums beating,
Oh, that's just my heart,
It's like deja vu, I feel the pain repeating,
I'm a good actor, in a bad movie, CUT! Let's take it from the start,
In my life I learned not to fear, but I shed tears,
This is my history, you may have heard of it,
Referred to as The Great Flood,
Could have done more right in my years, maybe I deserve it,
I need a house full of people that understand me,
So I can escape this deadly world of insanity,
I see hope in the glow of my baby girl's eyes,
I want to see from her point of view, because in my eyes all I see is lies.

Passion, Do I need to say more?

Untitled

The day that I first saw you, something told me there was something Special a bout you, how did I know,

That we would take a journey together in life, and it doesn't matter where We go,

Don't know where this river is going to take us, but we still follow the flow,

I don't care what's on this life screen as long as you are here with me to Watch the show,

You are such a beautiful person, I love your radiant glow.

Trouble Breathing

I can't believe that you are here with me, is this really happening,

I gotta look down at my chest to see if I'm still breathing, is this really happening,

The very sight of you takes my breath away, my chest gets tight, and my lungs began wheezing,

But I can't take my mind or my eyes off you, so pass me my asthma pump, cause I'm working hard to breathe and you are the main reason,

You're hot, beautiful and sexy from head to toe, look how you work your mind, body, and soul into one, you're so cold, I gotta catch you like its pneumonia season,

I need a doctor, will you be my doctor, it's a real easy job because I'm going to tell you what I need,

I need a oxygen tank, but take away the oxygen and fill the tank up with you,

This attack on my body is leaving me with a shortness of breath, and all I need is you to enter into my lungs and give me back me breath, if my life has any chance to succeed.

Miss u much

It's my first day back and it's not the same without you,
It seems so boring, quiet, I feel drained,
Never experienced it, but this could be torture, all I feel is pain,
Since you moved to that orange state, I feel nothing but blue,

You're down south where the weather is nice,
I'm left in this boring town, where are you, you were my excitement,
I'm searching for you like a buddhist searches for
Enlightenment,
I need your warmth, its so cold my car covered with frost and ice,

Memories of your smile and kindness,
Have me thinking about you constantly,
My brain is a slave to you, I'm mindless,
I wondered if she is feeling the same, tell me you do, honestly.

Passion

Your skin, my skin so different in appearance but put together
we make a desirable and similar motion,
You can smell the scent of my masculine and on top of you, I
smell your seductive lotion,
My body is warm, your body is warm so we create a heated
situation,
Extreme pleasure, ecstasy, and excitement is our one and only
destination,
We make music from this love which then creates beautiful
colors,
This is so much better than the gold at the end of the rainbow,
enough to make a leprechaun jealous,
Our bodies are actors and imitating the waves in the ocean,
Ours require detailed simulation,
I dedicate my time to satisfying your body with years of
devotion,
Your body, my body are magnets strongly attracted to each
other, our horoscope reads there will be no separation,
You began to learn my body and I began to study your spots,
It's all most time for the test,
Please remove everything off, you won't even need any paper or
pencil on your desk,
Your body, my body is like pieces of a puzzle that fit like a
perfect glove,
Your mind, my mind, my body, your body, your soul and my soul,
This connection is something special, had to be a gift sent
from the skies above,
This is the truth that was sent from God and will last an
eternity, we make fountain of youth love, it can never grow
old.

Move Your Mind

I'm going to take your mind on a roller coaster,

Getting scared, just hold me closer,
As we get higher and higher,

I know you feel my desire ,
To enter deep inside, past your stomach, to your mind,
I'm thorough with it, I can be in two parts of your body at one time,
Let's just start with the second one, that would have to be your spine,
The first one is you know, well lets just say I'm so kind,
Don't get me wrong, I want more than your sexy physique,
I want to take your mind, body, and soul on a trip that will last for an infinte number of weeks,
So pack your bags, its time to dip,
As this gentle Hercules moves your soul, like music moves your hips,
But enough about me, what's up with you, how you feel,
Did you know you move my spirit, it feels like I'm doing backflips and jumping jacks all
while I'm standing still,
Are you ready for this journey, are you ready for the real,
If not, don't even trip, we're better than Bonnie and Clyde

because we've got plenty of time to kill.

A well put together puzzle

You complete my thoughts, when I speak you finish my sentence, damn are we twins,
Your the canvas and I'm the paint brush, when put together we make beautiful art, we complete loopty loops, the rings in infinite have no ends,
When I'm not paying attention, you're always watching,
And when your asleep I'm awake,
I keep your brain fresh with oil like an engine, so you won't hear any knocking,
Sometimes I move at very high speeds, no fear, because you're a form of security to me like a break,
We fit together well, in place like a puzzle,
Soft spoken, but together we talk loud,
Our bite is as bad as our bark, you can't hold us back, can't contain us with no muzzle,
And like a plant, building and growing is our everyday hustle,
Individual, complicated thoughts but we understand each other,
And that why when we are together, we're a well put together puzzle.

IWonder

I wonder if she knows she's being undressed with my eyes,
I wonder if she knows that my hands will be undressing
    Her tonight,
I wonder if your body is as beautiful as my vivid
    Imagination has made it out to be,
I wonder can I be arrested for my explicit thoughts, it feels so
    Right,
I wonder if the sun is going to come up before we finish,
I wonder if our heat can warm this winter evening,
I wonder if your going to have the goose bumps this whole session,
I wonder if I'm going to need a air mask for this heavy breathing,
I wonder if you are ever going to find your panties and your skirt,
I wonder if I'm going to make it on time for work,
I wonder if I'm going to make it to work,
Forget it, I'm calling off.

Inhale

I want to smoke you, blow you away like the way you blew my mind away,

When I'm around you I see clearly, you don't lie to me, you always speak the truth,

You're not good for me, but you are,

When I inhale your essence, my pain you soothe,

You don't interrupt my thoughts, you help me you stay focus and think harder,
When I first met you I had trouble breathing,
Thanks to you I could put up my sax and my bass drum, cause I no longer have to sing the blues,
You're from or should I say your down to earth, so I dig you,
Submerged in your smoke, you're beautiful,
Too much to take in all at once, I choke,
You've taken a place in my mind, I hope the accomendations are suitable,
I inhale but I don't want to let you go, I don't want to exhale,
My eyes turn red with fury because I know that you can't stay,
Even now that your gone, you left your scent behind and it will linger on me for the rest of this beautiful day.

Untitled 3

You see my thoughts keep coming,
Hearing the sound of your voice, keeps my heart beat pumping,

Excitement and ecstasy,

Where did you come from, it keeps on vexing me,
How did you get here, your life is like a mystery,

Even if it takes awhile, I'll take the time to solve you,

Very complex but you being here is not even a problem,

My massage therapist, cause your conversation tends to soothe,

Promise me you'll always stay beautiful,

Now that's a word that decribes you from the core to the
outermost part of you skin,
So when it rains let me be your shelter then,

And come on out that bad weather,
Beautiful, the only thing about that word I don't agree with is
U and I aint together.

Poem 4U

I can't wait to touch you, can I touch you,
I'm like snow, sometimes I'm gentle but too much could crush you,

I want to explore every part of your body, from the top of your head to the bottom
Of your feet,
I want to get deep in your warmness until you have a tingle in your spine,
your legs get tired, and you have a numbness in your feet,
I want to get so deep that its like sitting in a class on some philosophy type shit,
Your body is a drug and I'm just getting out of rehabilitation, I can't take this,
I want to smoke it,
You got my mind racing at fast speeds, tongue twisted and tied tied and twisted,
A build up of excitement of anticipation of patiently waiting for our late night visit,
You are bad like Michael Jackson and your whole rersona is thrilling,
You always stay sharp these other girls are all dull they're boring just looking,
Damn you just stole my will power away from me, like a thief,
So sexy but you are more than that,
Damn I can't breathe,
Your my inhaler I'm waiting on you like I got an asthma attack.

Sexy

You're sexy as you want to be,

Look how you walk,
Your hips keep on taunting me,
I love how you talk,
I'm by myself and hope you come and bother me,
Your killing it, outlined in chalk,
Model that's super, come and save me,
Your like a wild tiger,
Yet elegant like a gazelle,
A good addiction, no other drug gets me higher,
Your heaven sent, you're like a cool breeze that came to
Bless this hot ass hell.

The Sun

The sun is warm and bright,

Without it there would be no life,

The sun gives us light to see,

Like the flashlight that shines to brighten up our night,
The sun is the center of our solar system,

The Earths source of energy,
The sun is always waiting behind the clouds to shine when days are
Dark,

I want you to be the sun in my life, but instead of being far away

Lets work on getting you close to me.

Special

If beauty is in the eye of the beholder, then you're like my eyelash that
Just feel in,
Get comfortable, I don't plan to take you out, but I plan to take you
Out and show the world and the treasure that lies beneath the
Surface, deep within,
But your not buried in the earth,
Priceless, Alicia Keys said it best when she said whats this women
Worth,
I want to hold you right now, come here and be my baby, let me
Cradle you,
I am everything you want, let me be everything you need, I'm more
Than capable,
So let us sit back and watch the world change, in all its
Variations,
Lay back on the ground and watch the sunset and make love under all the
Constellations,
I love being around you,
Its simply amazing.

UP,DOWN

Still miss you, thought it would be a little different when I woke up,
My emotions are confused, how is it that I'm still down now that I
Got up,
I feel like a deflated ballon, and you're like helium, I need you to help
Me get up,
I feel weak when I'm laying down, push the button, "Nurse can you come
Here to help me sit up",
Still miss you, thought it would be different when I woke up,

You're heavy in my head, you keep me grounded, hold me down,
Without you is like Battleship, I just been hit, I'm going down,
Weak knees, be my strength, I need you so I won't keep falling down,
You got me thinking, if I fell in the woods by myself would I make a sound
When I'm going down,
Many thoughts keep me up all night, be my anchor, I need some rest
Hold me down.

UNTITLED

I want to dress you in purple and call you my queen,

Thinking I can't stop, I'm a bad boy following his dream,

One look at you shuts my body down,
I hear everything you say and you didn't even make a sound,
Your beauty speaks loudly, it's very talkative,

For your love you got me waiting impatiently like a spoiled ass kid,

I can see into your future holding a strong man's hand,
I look at my past and how you saved me from sinking in chicken-heads like quick sand,
You're driving me crazy, like a new Ferrari baby,
You got my heart beat dancing to a disco beat, like we're living in the 80's,
One touch from you is too much excitement, it could create a baby,
You're like a piece of heaven, calm and sweet,
I bet your love could even make a Muslim eat red meat,
And they should cut off my hands now, cause I plan to steal your heart,
Excite your mental and insides, and give your body a jump start,
I feel an earthquake inside and it's measuring of the charts,
Too much for one, so I'm going into surgery to get a second heart,
This woman's worth,
This woman's work,
Makes a sinner want to go to church,
Makes a thief want to give,
Makes someone suicidal want to live,
But most importantly it makes me want you more,
It's like the feeling when an entrepreneur opens up his first store,
And I don't never want to close.

UNTITLED

You hold up my structure like the Great Egyptian's post and lintel,

When I thought I was going to stop, I thought more about you so I had to continue,
Everybody behind me is mad because I'm at the drive thru trying to order everything on your

menu,

A king and queen destine for the top,
When we enter on the scene, we heat up the spot,
When we vacate the premises, the room temperature seems to drop,
I just want to give you a little piece of my mind,
Baby I'm so happy, so glad your mine,
Trying to find another like you is like trying to find a needle in a haystack, very hard to find,
I'm going to always be there for you, you gotta luv dat,
Starring ain't my thing, but I love the way you make me act,
Me plus you is a combination that equals nothing but pure fact,
I'm the king of the hill, they can't knock me off, I'm going to always stand tall,
With my baby by my side, I can skate on thin ice and still be unable to fall,
Your beautiful like the point at the end of summer when it's about to turn into Fall,
I'm about to wrap this up and deal with the present,
The teacher is about to erase the board, and I hope you got everything from this lesson,
If you didn't, I'll be sure to give you a brief review in the next session.

Ur Voice

Everyday I look forward to hearing your beautiful seductive voice,

We were born with element to make our own decisions,
But when you talk I can't ignore you, I have to pay attention,

I have no choice,
It's full of sex appeal,
Refreshing like a orange you peel,
If I could decribe it in a song, it would have to be Babyface's Whip Appeal,
There is not enough words in the world to describe the feeling that you
Lovely voice makes me feel,
Your voice is so powerful I bet you could talk your way out of a thunderstorm,
Really,
Talk to me, tell me what you think, tell me how you feel, I need to hear it,
It doesn't matter it even be something silly,
You see, my ears are hungry and your voice fills their appetite,
You see, my ears don't have any eyes, they stay in the dark,
Your voice is the only time that they are able to see the light,

My ears don't have fingers, but they know that your voice has a soft delicate touch,

My ears do not have a nose, but if they did they would say that your voice is
Like smelling roses in a bunch,
But my ears can hear and I am pleased to have heard a sound so sweet,
Your voice is so strong that it's able to lift me right out of my seat,
So thank you God, for putting heaven in the form of sound,
Thank you for not keeping your voice to yourself,
I need your voice, its like a heartbeat to me, so vital to my health.

What's missing

If the sun don't shine, I want to take its place,
Even if no one else is running, I want to finish the race,
If there's no more air, I want to fill up your lungs,
I want to rock the show even if no comes,
I want to be the tick in the clock,
I want to be the donor that gives you the blood that makes your
Heart beat,

The force that makes you stand up for yourself, get you up out of

Your seat,

If there no more heat, I want to make the winters warm,

The eye of your tornado, calm in your storm,
I want to be what you're missing, the complete thought that finishes
Your fragmented sentence,

The drive that pushes you to finish your vision,

The decisiveness behind your decision,
The truth behind your stance, the honor behind your words,
I want to be the wind beneath your wings, that makes you soar
Higher than the birds,

If you don't have a pulse, I want to be the electricity that keeps you

Alive,

What more can I say.....

If you don't get it by now, I'll continue this on another day.

I Want2

I want to know you, get close to you like the tree branches reaching out to touch the sun,

I want to know you, know all about you, and when I finish start all over, keep it fresh ike we just begun,

I want to know you, get inside you like rain drops getting deep inside the ground,

I want to know you, get so close to you that our bodies get intermingled and we have one heart beat sound,

I want to know you, know every inch of you, to where I could draw a picture of your entire body from head to toe,

I want to know you, to where if you were a puzzle I could put you back together quickly wearing a blindfold,

I want to know you, get to know you, know your spots, get you to climax cool it down and when you are relaxed get you to climax once more,

I want to know you, know about all you have, like an owner taking inventory of his store,

I want to know you, get to know you, know what make you laugh, smile, cry, what makes your clock tick,

I want to know what makes you hungry for knowledge so I can feed your thought, I don't want to feed you bullshit that might make you sick.

Honey

Why am I attracted to you, is it your body, mind, and soul and just wondering if I were connected to all three how would it feel,

Or is it the fact that you have a anti-silicone perception, that means when you express your views, you always keep it real,
Can you feel the chemistry, they say that when two opposites come together they attract like two magnets,
This is a mystery, you have stolen my attention like some midnight bandits,
I feel like a little kid, I've got a crush on you,
But I'm not, I'm a grown man and I have vivid pictures of my hands touching you,
Smooth, chocolate coated candy skin, you sound like a dessert,
Sprinkled with a lot of intelligence, give me the works!
I'm attracted to you, like a bee to a flower, and the day is sunny,
Your nectar gives me the power to produce these sweet words written down, its like I'm writing honey.

Angel

Angel, don't ever leave my life,

You shine so bright, you give a blind man some sight,
You got a vise grip on my attention, that's why you are so tight,

Angel, don't ever disappear,

You're the backbone in my back, I stand straight and tall, I have no fear,

When I have rough times, I like how your hands are under my eyes the way you
Hold my tears,

Angel, don't ever leave my view,

Positive thoughts constantly and they are all about you,

You stay fresh in my head, expiration date says brand new,

Angel I need you to stay close to me. Please don't ever go nowhere.

I. WANT. U.

I. WANT. U.

I. WANT. U.

I. WANT. U. RIGHT. NOW. EVEN. THOUGH. U. LEFT. I. WANT. TO.
SEE. U. FEEL. U.
LISTEN. TO. THE. SOUND. U. MAKE. WHEN. U. TAKE. A. DEEP.
BREATH.

I. WANT. U. ON. TOP. OF. ME. OR. ME. ON. TOP. OF. U. BREATHING.
HEAVY. VERY.
SWEATY. AND. KEEP. UR. BODY. WARM. LIKE. THE. SUN. DO.

I. WANT. TO. LOOK. AT. U. LIKE. A. ARTIST. WHO. FINISHED. HIS.
MASTERPIECE. U.
R. A. MASTERPIECE.

I. WANT. U. LIKE. MUSEUMS. WANT. U. MONA. LISA. I. WANT. THE.
ONLY. SOUND. U. HEAR. IS. HEAVY. BREATHING. AND. ME. MOANING.
"LISA".

I. WANT. UR. SOFT. SKIN. RUBBING. AGAINST. MINE. I. WANT. MY.
PASSION. DEEP.
INSIDE. OF. U. SO. WHEN. U. GET. A. X-RAY. IT. SAYS. U. HAV. 2.
SPINES.

I. WANT. TO. SHOW. U. CAUSE. IT. WILL. BE. BETTER. THAN. I.
CAN. TEXT. U. I.
GOTTA. STOP. CAUSE. OF. THIS. THING. IN. MY. PANTS. IT. REALLY.

WANTS. TO. SEX. U.

www.ingramcontent.com/pod-product-compliance
Ingram Content Group UK Ltd.
Pitfield, Milton Keynes, MK11 3LW, UK
UKHW051136260726
13967UKWH00010B/3093